THE RUSSIAN MUSEUM, LENINGRAD

Painting

Painting

THE RUSSIAN MUSEUM, LENINGRAD

Aurora Art Publishers
Leningrad

Compiled and introduced
by **Nikolai Novouspensky**

Layout and design
by **Boris Osenchakov**

© **Aurora** Art Publishers, Leningrad, 1988

Printed and bound in the USSR

$\Gamma \dfrac{4903020000\text{-}726}{023(01)\text{-}88}$ 24-88

ISBN 5-7300-0254-8

The Russian Museum in Leningrad is a world-famous repository of Russian art. It houses more than 300,000 items, including numerous samples of old Russian arts and handicrafts, painting and sculpture, thousands of drawings, watercolours and engravings and, finally, priceless works of decorative and applied art. Its collection of paintings (nearly 14,000 in number) boasts magnificent canvases by the most prominent artists, reflecting the history of Russian art from the twelfth century to the present day.

In March 1898, the first state museum of Russian art was opened in the Mikhailovsky Palace, one of the most illustrious architectural monuments of the Russian Empire style, built in 1819—25 to the design of Carlo Rossi (he was also responsible for the interior decoration of the palace). In the 1930s, the adjacent building, put up at the turn of the century to the design of Leonty Benois, was assigned to the Museum for use as an exhibition hall. The rooms of the so-called Rossi wings, originally occupied by the palace's maintenance services, were also converted into show-rooms. To this day the collections of the Russian Museum are housed here, but great changes have taken place in their composition and in the exhibition now laid out in 120 rooms.

To begin with, the Museum's collection of paintings numbered only 445 pieces. It consisted of works by Russian artists which had been transferred from the Museum of the Academy of Arts and the Hermitage, from royal palaces and private collections. Although for this reason various periods, trends and the work of the major artists were unevenly represented in the Museum, its inauguration, in 1898, was a significant event in the cultural life of the whole country. In the very first year it was visited by more than 100,000 people.

After the October Revolution, thousands of wonderful works of art entered the Museum from palaces, mansions and country estates. New departments of decorative and applied art, and of folk art were established. The department of Soviet art gradually became one of the largest in the Museum. For the first time the display was organized on scientific and historical principles. The Museum was gradually being transformed into a truly scientific institution.

The 161 paintings included in this edition illustrate the main stages in the development of Russian artistic culture. The book opens with reproductions of icons executed eight hundred years ago and concludes with canvases by contemporary artists.

The reforms which were effected during the early eighteenth century to reshape feudal Russia, the difficult wars against foreign invaders and the country's tempestuous development were all factors that contributed to the emergence of realistic art in Russia, an art which centred attention on man and his spiritual world. This naturally led to the predominance of the portrait genre which attained great heights in the eighteenth century thanks to the contribution made by a pleiad of outstanding masters.

The first experiments in portrait painting are connected with the so-called *parsunas* of the end of the seventeenth century. A typical example is the *Portrait of Andrei Apraxin, Peter the Great's Jester*. The laconic individual characterization combines here with a somewhat conventional, flat treatment of the image that shows the unknown artist's familiarity with the long-established technique of icon painting.

Works by artists of a later period also bore the imprint of the icon tradition: this may be illustrated by the *Portrait of Maria Stroganova* by Roman Nikitin.

In the 1720s, however, there emerged a new, realistic type of portraiture. Two of the most outstanding exponents of this novel style of the Petrine epoch were Ivan Nikitin and Andrei Matveyev. Both were sent abroad by Peter I to perfect their skills there. Having mastered the techniques of Western European painting, they lost none of their own artistic individuality.

Nikitin's portrait of Peter I, though extremely laconic in treatment, faithfully recreates the image of this forceful personality. In the pair portrait of Andrei Matveyev and his wife one senses a warm sincerity beneath the outward signs of the epoch—the rather affected poses and stereotyped gestures. Executed in the 1750s by Ivan Vishniakov, the childhood portrait of Sarah-Eleanor Fermore has a light, poetic aura about it.

In spite of the fact that the prevailing atmosphere in the royal court and the salons of the aristocracy was one of mannerism, the best Russian painters managed to rise above the glitter of court etiquette and penetrate the inner world of their subjects. This is true above all of the great Russian portraitists Fiodor

Rokotov, Dmitry Levitsky and Vladimir Borovikovsky. The technical perfection of their paintings goes hand in hand with their meaningful profundity and humanism. Levitsky reproduced with unsurpassed skill the beautiful satins and velvets of the rich garments, but this is by no means his principal achievement—his portraits depict concrete people endowed with characters and emotions peculiarly their own.

In his portraits, Borovikovsky was able to convey the subject's fleeting emotions and pensive, visionary moods, to capture the delicate nuances of feeling. The artist frequently introduced landscapes into his works which played an important role in character-drawing.

Though the eighteenth century in Russian art was to a great extent the age of the portrait, it saw the emergence of other genres as well. The works of Fiodor Matveyev and Semion Shchedrin heralded the birth of landscape painting. At the turn of the eighteenth and nineteenth centuries, Fiodor Alexeyev broke away from the canons of "scenic" painting and created the first townscapes: he is at his exquisite best in those of his canvases which reflect the beauty and lyric harmony of St Petersburg. Sylvester Shchedrin produced poetic pictures of Italy, alive with its humid air and gentle mountain haze.

In the thirties and forties of the nineteenth century, Alexander Ivanov, working on his immense canvas *Christ Appearing before the People*, executed numerous preliminary studies. The artist's craftsmanship is so extraordinary, his technique so perfect, his penetration into man's spiritual world so deep that these studies can be regarded as remarkable works in their own right. They represent the first ever attempt in the history of Russian art to tackle the problems of plein-air painting.

The genre of history painting made its début in Russia in the eighteenth century and by its end had grown to be the dominant form. The decisive factor here was the inauguration in St Petersburg in 1757 of the Academy of Arts, which for some eighty years remained the only institution in the country to turn out professionally trained artists. The Academy became the focal point in the implementation of official policy concerning the fine arts. It stood for an exalted art of great ideological content, inculcating patriotism and a sense of civic duty.

The genre of history painting seemed to best serve this purpose. The history of every nation can yield many examples of heroic exploits, noble deeds and self-sacrifice on the part of its outstanding personalities. Students of the Academy were encouraged to treat these themes in their works. Since the classical doctrine was predominant in art academies the world over, it was natural for the St Petersburg Academy to adhere to it as well.

Academic art engendered a number of characteristic conventions: it was rationalistic, based on strict rules of drawing, composition and colour scheme. In their quest for heroic themes, the academicians turned to events and legends of classical antiquity, trying to imitate the classics of the Italian Renaissance.

The merits and shortcomings of classicism were fully typical for the Russian academic school of painting. It was quite often, however, that eminent artists introduced contemporary national problems into the historic and mythological subjects of their canvases.

One of the first pupils of the Academy of Arts and its first professor, Anton Losenko painted his picture *Vladimir and Rogneda* on a subject from Russian history. Although the artist treated the theme rather conventionally and his main hero, Prince Vladimir, thus resembles a personage from a gallant theatrical scene, there are certain purely Russian elements in the picture; some heroes are even endowed with distinctly popular features.

The growth of national consciousness and the upsurge of patriotic feelings, brought about by the 1812 War, laid an imprint on the historic canvases executed at that time. Fiodor Bruni's canvas *Death of Camilla, Sister of Horatius*, painted one year before the Decembrists' Revolt, may serve as a good example. This work, an outstanding achievement of Russian classicism, carries evocations of true patriotism and self-sacrifice for the sake of the people.

As a rule, the strengthening of the democratic tendencies in the social consciousness of a nation is accompanied by the flourishing of realism in art. This tendency also manifested itself in the history of nineteenth century Russian culture. One of the most notable artists active in the first half of the nineteenth century was Orest Kiprensky. While developing the finest traditions of eighteenth century portraitists, he accentuated in his sitters the nobility of spirit and strength of emotion. Many of Kiprensky's portraits are imbued with a feeling of romantic uplift. In that same period a new page in the history of Russian art was opened by Alexei Venetsianov. He created images of Russian peasants, full of spiritual power, poetry and beauty, which should by no means be seen as mere "imitations of nature", as the artist used to say. The unprecedented development of Russian genre painting began with Venetsianov's small-size canvases in which he took the common people as his main heroes. He was the first in Russian painting to produce lyrical rural landscapes.

As time went on, the fresh breeze of realism penetrated even the Academy of Arts, forcing its most gifted students to overstep the boundaries of the aesthetic standards imposed on them. This is especially evident in the works of Karl Briullov. Greatly impressed by what he saw at archaeological excavations near Naples, Briullov painted his gigantic canvas *The Last Day of Pompeii*, in which a tragedy of the distant past, the destruction of the city by the eruption of Mt. Vesuvius, is reproduced with tremendous force. Striving for historical authenticity, Briullov made the characters, actions and emotions of his subjects the leitmotif of the composition, emphasizing the strength and noble dignity of human feeling. The people in Briullov's masterpiece are beautiful, but this is not because he borrowed their likenesses from ancient statues, which was the usual practice among the artists of the academic school. He perceived beauty in the features of the Italians of his day, sketching them from nature. This explains the all-pervading vibrancy and dynamism of the picture, this is why it produces such a powerful impact even on the modern viewer.

Romantic tendencies are also apparent in the oeuvre of the outstanding Russian seascape painter Ivan Aivazovsky. The motifs of his paintings were shipwrecks, storms, man's struggle with the majestic and ominous elements, or the magic charm of a moonlit sea. His works are distinguished by an emotional intensity and solemn beauty.

In the mid-nineteenth century, a contemporary of Briullov, the incomparable Pavel Fedotov, was responsible for the emergence of critical realism in painting, a trend which determined the entire development of Russian artistic culture in the second half of the nineteenth century. In his small-size but astonishingly cogent canvases devoted to the everyday life of the "little man", in the dramatic, at times comic situations of his pieces, in his typological characterizations, Fedotov revealed the significance of social phenomena just prior to the upsurge of the liberation movement in Russia. His *Major's Marriage Proposal*, for example, is at first glance only a family scene, rather curious and a bit funny. But behind the all too obvious interrelationships of the personages one can descry whole social groups and classes, their typical traits and even their historical destinies. Although the scene is presented in a humorous vein, the spectator is stirred to active meditation. This applies to every one of Fedotov's thematic canvases, only his humour would sometimes give way to great commiseration for human suffering and condemnation of injustice. Fedotov loved people and was highly sensitive to the beauty and kindness inherent in them. His portrait miniatures vividly express this attitude, as is exemplified by the charming image of Nadezhda Zhdanovich at the piano.

The democratic ideals of the time were very clearly reflected in the oeuvre of Vasily Perov. His painting *A Meal in the Monastery* is a scathing denunciation of church morals.

The year 1870 saw the formation of the Society for Circulating Art Exhibitions, and a year later, in December 1871, it held its first exhibition. This was an event of the utmost significance not only in the artistic, but also in the social life of Russia. The movement of the Itinerants, as they were called, became synonymous with all that was progressive in the fine arts of the country. Champions of truth and humanism, the Itinerants focused attention on the everyday life of the people, their joys and sorrows, their present and past, their struggle for a happier future.

The ideological leader of the Itinerants, Ivan Kramskoi, worked mainly in the portrait genre and produced a whole gallery of his contemporaries from the intelligentsia and the peasantry. The *Portrait of the Painter Ivan Shishkin* and *Mina Moiseyev* reproduced in this book, rate among the best of his creations.

The Itinerants introduced a new approach to the then widespread religious motif in painting. Thus, in *The Last Supper* by Nikolai Gay, one of the Society's founder-members, the evangelical legend is treated as a moral human drama.

The Itinerants and other like-minded artists glorified the unfading beauty of the rural scene. Conventional landscapes acquired in their canvases both poetic meaning and social colouring. An important contribution to the development of Russian landscape painting was made by Alexei Savrasov. His works combine impeccable mastery with spontaneity of vision (*View of the Moscow Kremlin. Spring*).

By the purity and power of their colours, the emotional, romantically elevated pictures of Fiodor Vasilyev, a talented artist who died too soon, came as a real revelation for the 1870s. His *Scene on the Volga. Barques* is a passionate hymn of praise to the radiant enchantment of a summer morning on the Volga.

The Russian forest was the subject of the monumental canvases of Ivan Shishkin, who devoted himself to extolling the majestic wealth of Russian nature. Among his finest works is the *Mast-tree Grove* reproduced here.

The legacy of Arkhip Kuinji occupies a place apart in Russian art. This unique master's forte were the effects of lighting. Vivid sunsets, rainbows, the dazzling sunlight piercing the green birches or eternal snows are the main themes of his works.

All the finest achievements of the Itinerants in landscape painting were concentrated in the eighties and nineties in the oeuvre of Isaac Levitan, a pupil and follower of Savrasov and Polenov. He created so-called mood landscapes in which the image of nature is animated with human emotions. Levitan's artistic vocabulary is extraordinarily simple and subtle. His canvas *The Lake. Russia* completed by and large the evolution of Russian landscape painting in the second half of the nineteenth century. It is a poem about Russia in all its unadorned beauty and solemn grandeur.

The major Russian artists of the second half of the nineteenth century, Ilya Repin and Vasily Surikov, embodied in their canvases the most salient features of the art of the Itinerants.

A brilliant painter and draughtsman, Repin left to posterity a large number of portraits, historic canvases and genre pictures notable for their powerful imagery and profound philosophical insight. Repin's portraits constitute an extensive gallery of his contemporaries. It was in this genre that his genius manifested itself most vividly. His portrait of the art critic Vladimir Stasov, who waged a struggle for realism in art, is one of his best creations. The very manner of its execution seems to convey the passionate character of the model. The portrait of Pobedonostsev, one of the most bitter enemies of freedom in Russia, is painted in an entirely different way: a broad but dwindling brushstroke captures the pallid, corpse-like features and cold expression of Pobedonostsev's face.

In Repin's *The Zaporozhye Cossacks Writing a Mocking Letter to the Turkish Sultan*, the story of the seventeenth century free Cossacks is, as it were, brought to life. The sweeping brushstrokes are no less expressive of the life-asserting spirit of the picture than the figures of the Cossacks themselves.

In his canvases Surikov showed an entirely novel approach to history in that he believed it to be the result of actions by the popular masses. The spirit of bygone times is resurrected by the artist in *The Taking of a Snow Fortress*, in which the imagery and brushwork are radiant and full of the joy of living.

The development of Russian art in the second half of the nineteenth century was crowned by a number of outstanding realistic paintings.

In the 1880s, Russian art stood at the threshold of a qualitatively new period in its evolution. This was a result of Russia entering the stage of imperialism, whose characteristic features were sharp social conflicts and an ensuing struggle of ideas. The progressive artistic intelligentsia's deeply embedded democratic traditions were the main factors which helped the artists stand firm on their realistic platform and create a vivid, diverse and original art.

One of the major artists of this period was Valentin Serov, a pupil of Repin. He created real masterpieces in all genres of pictorial art, particularly portrait painting. Whatever subject he took up, he would lay bare its immanent character with acute insight, poetic force and unmatched artistry. His images are at times mellow and romantic, at times relentlessly sarcastic, but always based on a comprehensive and subtle awareness of life's truth.

Mikhail Vrubel carried the viewer away into the world of the fairytale, folklore and the poetry of Pushkin and Lermontov. The exalted, symbolic images of his pictures are charged with deep philosophic power and are full of an inner tension. Vrubel's painting is possessed of a beauty, integrity and expressiveness all its own, and his colours sparkle like precious stones, reflecting both the loveliness of the universe and his own spiritual generosity.

Alexander Benois, Konstantin Somov, and Evgeny Lanceray, three of the most prominent members of the World of Art group (a society which played a vital role in the development of turn-of-the century art), devoted themselves largely to poeticizing the past. They were particularly fond of depicting the architecture and landscape gardens of seventeenth century France and eighteenth century Russia, and had a precise and penetrating eye for their specific charm. At times the elegant pictures of these artists bear a trace of the ironic, and this is especially true of Somov's works. The World of Art members were also very active in book illustration and popularized Russian art in Western European countries by designing stage sets and costumes for the Russian Ballet Seasons in Paris.

While speaking of the early twentieth century artists whose works are on show in the Russian Museum, mention should be made of Abram Arkhipov, a follower of the tradition of the Itinerants; Alexander Golovin, that great master of theatrical decor; Philip Maliavin, the author of vivid canvases devoted to Russian rural life; Nikolai Roerich, an archaeologist and painter whose works abound in fantastic symbols; Boris Kustodiev and Konstantin Yuon, poets of the Russian provincial scene; Victor Borisov-Musatov who combined in his oeuvre a realistic portrayal of life and symbolism; and Ilya Mashkov, the author of vibrant, glowing still lifes so Russian in spirit. This list is in itself sufficiently indicative of the diversity of Russian art in the pre-revolutionary years. The works of these masters served as a bridge which spanned post-revolutionary Russian and Soviet art. With the establishment of the new social system these talented artists contributed to the creation of the art of socialist realism, an art varied in form but united in ideological content.

In the first years after the Revolution, works were produced which depicted the heroic reality of the period, the new way of life and the changes that were effected in the country. Thus, in 1921, Kustodiev painted a large decorative canvas called *Festivities Marking the Opening of the Second Congress of the Comintern and Demonstration on Uritsky (Palace) Square in Petrograd on July 19, 1920*, in which by stressing the rhythmic play of colours and employing the techniques of stage decor he convincingly recreated the atmosphere of a revolutionary holiday enlivened by the people's joy at their newly found freedom.

Especially interesting and significant was the work of Kuzma Petrov-Vodkin. In 1928 he created his canvas, *Death of a Commissar*, in which he found a philosophic solution to a subject linked with the Civil War in Russia.

In the thirties, the ranks of Soviet artists were reinforced by a number of young masters who had received their training at Soviet art schools.

In 1932, the Union of Soviet Artists was formed, uniting under its auspices masters of various artistic groups. The building of socialism and the life itself were posing new tasks before art: many artists devoted themselves to historico-revolutionary themes and portraiture. It was especially important to show the active, creative nature of Soviet men and women. A typical example is the *Portrait of the Surgeon Sergei Yudin* by Mikhail Nesterov, one of the oldest Soviet artists. The transformation which the work of this outstanding master underwent during his later years is symbolic. It reflects the overall evolution of Russian art after October 1917. Whereas in the pre-revolutionary period Nesterov had won renown for his lyrical treatment of religious motifs, after the Revolution he attained remarkable success as a portrait painter whose images were always realistic, comprehensive and life-asserting.

The work of Soviet artists in the late 1920s and 1930s was neither one-sided nor stereotyped. Suffice it to mention yet another outstanding piece of portraiture of those years, *Young Woman Worker* by Alexander Samokhvalov. It is a synthetic portrayal of the Soviet youth during the reconstruction period and the early stages of socialist construction.

The ordeals which the Soviet Union underwent during the War of 1941—45 did not arrest the development of art. The war gave birth to powerful paintings imbued with patriotism and emotional force. One of the most significant canvases of the period is Alexander Deineka's *The Defence of Sevastopol*. In a life-and-death fight between the Black Sea sailors and the Nazis the artist conveyed the spirit of the irreconcilable, relentless struggle of the entire Soviet people against the Nazi invaders. The ideological content of the canvas is revealed with the utmost tension and laconicism.

Arkady Plastov's depiction of man's daily life and toil is coloured by a poetic vision of nature. The principal motif of his canvases is the new life of the collective farmer. Rich, lush colours and succulent brushstrokes characterize his pictures *Youth* and *Vitia the Shepherd-boy*.

The plates reproduced on the last pages of this book illustrate the creative endeavour of Soviet artists of the recent period and testify to their achievements.

As far back as the thirties and forties, Semion Chuikov, a subtle lyrical artist and colourist, created magnificent poetic images of the people and scenery of Soviet Kirghizia. To this day it is his favourite theme. In the fifties Chuikov painted a series of pictures devoted to India.

In his painting *Cherries*, the Leningrad artist Evsey Moiseyenko, developed the principal theme of his work, the heroic period of the Civil War. The representational structure of the canvas is rhythmically complex and extremely generalized. A different treatment is present in Gely Korzhev-Chuveliov's canvas *Homer (Workers' Studio)*. By means of frugal and well-observed details, the artist creates a highly impressive image. In all his works Korzhev-Chuveliov asserts the finest aspects of the popular character and brings out the inner strength of the Soviet people. He is attracted to images of his contemporaries and ponders a great deal on their lives and destinies.

The tendency to amalgamate in one canvas elements of genre painting, portrait and landscape is characteristic of the 1960s—80s. This widens the representational framework of the picture, enabling the artists to delve deeper into the manifold and interrelated laws of life. The striving to reveal the active, dynamic and typical qualities of man often transforms a portrait into a picture. On the other hand, personages in genre paintings acquire the expressiveness of a portrait, which tends to make these works particularly convincing. The *Sisters* by Andrei Mylnikov and *Rebirth* by Boris Ugarov may serve as examples.

The works created in this period by Gely Korzhev-Chuveliov, Victor Ivanov, Victor Popkov, Piotr Ossovsky and other talented artists are distinguished by their civic pathos and bold affirmation of the beauty and moral strength of the Soviet people—the most fundamental features of contemporary Soviet men and women reflected in their daily activities and, consequently, in the entire Soviet way of life. A general picture is thereby achieved without blurring the essential characteristics of the subject.

The canvases by Soviet artists reproduced in this book will acquaint the reader with the development of Soviet art and the individual pictorial idiom of the most outstanding of its representatives.

The wealth and diversity of the Russian Museum's collection, and the constant research into the legacy of many generations of Russian artists, carefully preserved by the people, shed a new light on the artistic treasures of the past and help reveal the distinctive features of Soviet art.

Nikolai Novouspensky

Plates

1. ARCHANGEL GABRIEL
(Angel with Golden Hair). 12th century

2. THE MIRACLE OF ST GEORGE
Novgorod school. Last quarter of the 15th century

3. THE PRESENTATION IN THE TEMPLE
Novgorod school. First half of the 14th century

4. THE DESCENT INTO LIMBO. 1502—3
Dionysius' workshop

5. THE OLD TESTAMENT TRINITY
Novgorod school. Mid-16th century

6. PORTRAIT OF PRINCE IVAN REPNIN.
Second half of the 17th century

7. UNKNOWN ARTIST
Active first quarter of the 18th century
Portrait of Andrei Apraxin, Peter the Great's Jester

8. IVAN NIKITIN
Portrait of Sergei Stroganov. 1726

9. ROMAN NIKITIN
Portrait of Maria Stroganova. Between 1721 and 1724

10. ANDREI MATVEYEV
Self-Portrait of the Artist with His Wife. 1729 (?)

11. IVAN NIKITIN
Portrait of Peter I. First half of the 1720s

12. IVAN ARGUNOV
Portrait of Ekaterina Lobanova-Rostovskaya. 1754

13. ALEXEI ANTROPOV
Portrait of Fiodor Krasnoshchokov. 1761

14. IVAN ARGUNOV
Portrait of an Unknown Sculptor (Architect?). 1760s

15. IVAN VISHNIAKOV
Portrait of Sarah-Eleanor Fermore. 1750s

16. FIODOR ROKOTOV
Portrait of Ivan Orlov. Between 1762 and 1765

17. DMITRY LEVITSKY
Portrait of Alexander Kokorinov. 1769

18. FIODOR ROKOTOV
Portrait of Varvara Surovtseva. Second half of the 1780s

19. FIODOR ROKOTOV
Portrait of Elizaveta Santi. 1785

20. ANDREI IVANOV
Kiev Youth's Act of Bravery during the Siege
of Kiev by the Pechenegs in 968. *C*. 1810

21. ANTON LOSENKO
Vladimir and Rogneda. 1770

22. VLADIMIR BOROVIKOVSKY
Portrait of Fiodor Borovsky. 1799

23. VLADIMIR BOROVIKOVSKY
Portrait of Ekaterina Arsenyeva. Second half of the 1790s

24. DMITRY LEVITSKY
Portrait of Ekaterina Molchanova. 1776

25. DMITRY LEVITSKY
Portrait of Ekaterina Nelidova. 1773

26. FIODOR MATVEYEV
View of the Lake of Bolsena in Italy. 1819

27. SYLVESTER SHCHEDRIN
Mergellina in Naples. 1827

28. FIODOR ALEXEYEV
View of the Peter and Paul Fortress and Palace Embankment in St Petersburg. 1799

29. FIODOR ALEXEYEV
View of the English Embankment from Vasilyevsky Island in St Petersburg

30. KARL BRIULLOV
Self-Portrait. Repetition of the 1848 *Self-Portrait*

31. OREST KIPRENSKY
Portrait of Adam Schwalbe, the Artist's Father. 1804

32. KARL BRIULLOV
Italian Midday (An Italian Woman Gathering Grapes). 1827

33. KARL BRIULLOV
Portrait of Countess Julia Samoilova Leaving the Ball. Not later than 1842

34. FIODOR BRUNI
Death of Camilla, Sister of Horatius. 1824

35. KARL BRIULLOV
The Last Day of Pompeii. 1833

36. VASILY TROPININ
The Solitary Guitar Player (Portrait of Pavel Vasilyev). 1830s

37. OREST KIPRENSKY
Portrait of Karl Albrecht. 1827

38. ALEXEI VENETSIANOV
Girl with a Birch-bark Jar. *C.* 1824

39. ALEXEI VENETSIANOV
Sleeping Shepherd-boy. Between 1823 and 1826

40. GRIGORY SOROKA
The Study in a Country House at Ostrovki. 1844

41. NIKIFOR KRYLOV
Winter Landscape (Russian Winter). 1827

42. PAVEL FEDOTOV
Portrait of Nadezhda Zhdanovich at the Piano. 1849

43. PAVEL FEDOTOV
The Major's Marriage Proposal. 1851

44. IVAN AIVAZOVSKY
View of Odessa on a Moonlit Night. 1846

45. IVAN AIVAZOVSKY
The Brig *Mercury*. 1848

46. ALEXANDER IVANOV
Tree in the Shadow above the Water in the Vicinity
of Castel Gandolfo. Not earlier than 1846

47. ALEXANDER IVANOV
Three Naked Boys. 1840—50s. Study for the painting *Christ Appearing before the People*. 1833—57

48. ALEXANDER IVANOV
Head of John the Baptist. Study for the painting
Christ Appearing before the People. 1833—57

49. NIKOLAI GAY
The Last Supper. 1863

50. IVAN KRAMSKOI
Portrait of the Sculptor Mark Antokolsky. 1876

51. NIKOLAI GAY
Peter the Great Interrogating Tsarevich Alexei in Peterhof. 1872

52. IVAN KRAMSKOI
Mina Moiseyev. 1882. Study for the painting of 1883, *Peasant with a Bridle*

53. IVAN KRAMSKOI
Portrait of the Painter Ivan Shishkin. 1880

54. ALEXEI SAVRASOV
View of the Moscow Kremlin. Spring. 1873

55. FIODOR VASILYEV
The Thaw. 1871

56. FIODOR VASILYEV
Scene on the Volga. Barques. 1870

57. GRIGORY MIASOYEDOV
The Mowers. 1887

58. VASILY PEROV
A Meal in the Monastery. 1865—76

59. LEONID SOLOMATKIN
Petrouchka. 1878

60. ARKHIP KUINJI
Evening in the Ukraine. 1878

61. IVAN SHISHKIN
Mast-tree Grove. 1898

62. ISAAC LEVITAN
Golden Autumn. Village. 1889

63. ISAAC LEVITAN
The Lake. Russia. 1899—1900

64. ISAAC LEVITAN
Meadow on the Edge of a Forest. 1898

65. VASILY POLENOV
In the Park. The Village of Veules in Normandy. 1874

66. VASILY POLENOV
Christ and the Woman Sinner. 1888

67. VASILY VERESHCHAGIN
The Shinto Temple in Nikko. 1903

68. VASILY SURIKOV
The Taking of a Snow Fortress. 1891

69. VASILY SURIKOV
Suvorov's Army Crossing the Alps in 1799. 1899

70. ILYA REPIN
Portrait of Vladimir Stasov, Music and Art Critic. 1883

71. ILYA REPIN
Portrait of the Cellist Alexander Verzhbilovich. 1895

72. ILYA REPIN
The Volga Barge Haulers. 1870—73

73. ILYA REPIN
The Zaporozhye Cossacks Writing a Mocking Letter to the Turkish Sultan. 1880—91

74. ILYA REPIN
Portrait of Konstantin Pobedonostsev. Study for the painting
The State Council in Formal Session. 1903

75. VALENTIN SEROV
Children. 1899

76. VALENTIN SEROV
Portrait of Felix Yusupov. 1903

77. VALENTIN SEROV
Portrait of Sophia Botkina. 1899

78. KONSTANTIN SOMOV
Portrait of Anna Ostroumova. 1901

79. MIKHAIL NESTEROV
Portrait of Olga Nesterova, the Artist's Daughter. 1906

80. MIKHAIL VRUBEL
The Bogatyr. Decorative panel. 1898

81. MIKHAIL VRUBEL
Six-winged Seraph. 1904

82. LEON BAKST
Portrait of Sergei Diaghilev with His Nurse. 1906

83. MIKHAIL NESTEROV
The Taking of the Veil. 1898

84. KONSTANTIN KOROVIN
The Harbour in Gurzuf. 1914

85. KONSTANTIN KOROVIN
Portrait of the Actress Tatyana Liubatovich

86. VICTOR BORISOV-MUSATOV
Self-Portrait of the Artist with His Sister. 1898

87. VICTOR BORISOV-MUSATOV
Spring. 1901

88. EVGENY LANCERAY
St Petersburg in the Early Eighteenth Century. 1906

89. KONSTANTIN SOMOV
Winter. Skating-rink. 1915

90. KONSTANTIN YUON
The St Trinity Lavra in Winter. 1910

91. PHILIP MALIAVIN
Two Peasant Women. 1905

92. ANDREI RIABUSHKIN
A Seventeenth-century Moscow Street on a Holiday. 1895

93. ABRAM ARKHIPOV
A Festive Day in Spring (On a Visit). 1915

94. APOLLINARY VASNETSOV
Seventeenth-century Moscow. Street in Kitai-gorod. 1900

95. VICTOR VASNETSOV
Vitiaz (Knight) at the Crossroads. 1882

96. NIKOLAI ROERICH
Slavs on the Dnieper. 1905

97. NIKOLAI ROERICH
St Prokopius. 1914

98. ALEXANDER GOLOVIN
A Street in Seville. Sketch of the stage set for Bizet's opera *Carmen.* 1906

99. ALEXANDER GOLOVIN
Portrait of Fiodor Shaliapin as Boris Godunov
in Mussorgsky's opera of the same name. 1912

100. IGOR GRABAR
Still Life with Pears. 1915

101. IGOR GRABAR
Flowers and Fruit. 1904

102. ZINAIDA SEREBRIAKOVA
A House of Cards. 1919

103. ZINAIDA SEREBRIAKOVA
Study of a Girl (Self-Portrait). 1911

104. ZINAIDA SEREBRIAKOVA
Peasants. 1914

105. KUZMA PETROV-VODKIN
A Mother. 1915

106. BORIS KUSTODIEV
A Merchant's Wife Drinking Tea. 1918

107. BORIS KUSTODIEV
Portrait of Fiodor Shaliapin. 1922

108. ILYA MASHKOV
Still Life with Loaves of Bread

109. PIOTR KONCHALOVSKY
Family Portrait. 1911

110. ALEXANDER KUPRIN
Still Life with Blue Fan. 1919

111. NATHAN ALTMAN
Portrait of Anna Akhmatova. 1914

112. ROBERT FALK
The Crimea. Lombardy Poplar. 1915

113. MARK CHAGALL
The Promenade. 1917

114. KASIMIR MALEVICH
Marpha and Van'ka. 1909—10

115. DAVID STERENBERG
Still Life with Oil Lamp. *C.* 1922

116. VASILY ROZHDESTVENSKY
Still Life with Red Jug. 1918

117. KUZMA PETROV-VODKIN
Violin. 1918

118. KONSTANTIN YUON
Young People of the Moscow Suburbs. 1926

119. BORIS KUSTODIEV
Festivities Marking the Opening of the Second Congress
of the Comintern and Demonstration on Uritsky (Palace) Square
in Petrograd on July 19, 1920. 1921

120. FIODOR BOGORODSKY
At the Photographer's. 1932

121. KUZMA PETROV-VODKIN
Death of a Commissar. 1928

122. ARKADY RYLOV
Wind in the Trees. 1904

123. ARKADY RYLOV
Autumn on the Tosna River. 1920

124. MARTIROS SARYAN
Yerevan. 1924

125. MARTIROS SARYAN
Hyenas. 1909

126. ALEXANDER SHEVCHENKO
Kurd Women. 1932—33

127. ALEXANDER SHEVCHENKO
Girl with Pears. 1933

128. NIKOLAI CHERNYSHOV
Young Collective Farmer (Girl with a Kid). 1929

129. PAVEL KUZNETSOV
Tobacco-workers. 1925—26

130. ALEXANDER SAMOKHVALOV
Young Woman Worker. 1928

131. ALEXANDER SAMOKHVALOV
Weavers. 1929

132. SERGEI GERASIMOV
Autumntide. 1953

133. ALEXANDER GERASIMOV
Midday. Warm Rain. 1939

134. YURI PIMENOV
Portrait of Varia Shitakova. 1935

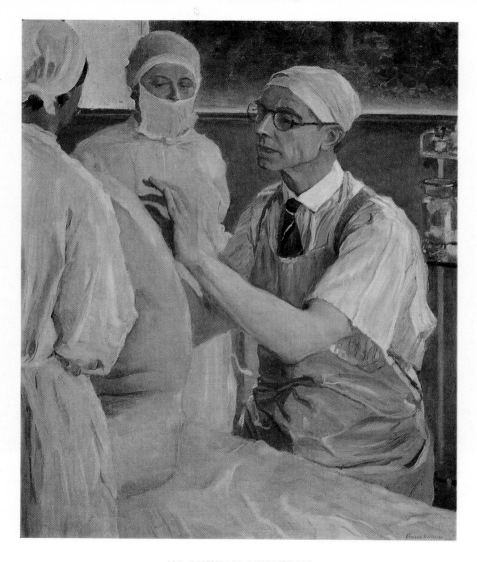

135. MIKHAIL NESTEROV
Portrait of the Surgeon Sergei Yudin. 1933

136. PIOTR KONCHALOVSKY
The Novgorodians. 1925

137. GEORGY RIAZHSKY
Self-Portrait. 1928

138. ALEXANDER DEINEKA
La Parisienne. 1935

139. ALEXANDER DEINEKA
Mont Vernon. The Highway. 1935

140. ALEXANDER OSMIORKIN
The "New Holland" Arch. 1945

141. ALEXEI KAREV
The Neva. 1934

142. THE KUKRYNIKSY
The Nazis Being Routed from Novgorod. 1944—46

143. ALEXANDER DEINEKA
The Defence of Sevastopol. 1942

144. ARKADY PLASTOV
Youth. 1954

145. ARKADY PLASTOV
Vitia the Shepherd-boy. 1951

146. YURI PIMENOV
Venice. A Lonely Flower Girl. 1958

147. YURI PIMENOV
Trend-setters of a New District. From the *New District* series. 1961

148. SEMION CHUIKOV
The Song of a Coolie. Central panel of the triptych *Simple People of India*. 1959

149. SEMION CHUIKOV
Morning in a Mountain Village. 1967

150. GEORGY NISSKY
Above the Snows. 1960

151. PAVEL KORIN
Portrait of Renato Guttuso. 1961

152. EVSEI MOISEYENKO
Cherries. 1969

153. EVSEI MOISEYENKO
Victory. 1970—72

154. GELY KORZHEV-CHUVELIOV
Homer (Workers' Studio). Left-hand panel
of the triptych *Communists*. 1957—60

155. BORIS UGAROV
Rebirth. 1980

156. PIOTR OSSOVSKY
Gantry Grane. 1965

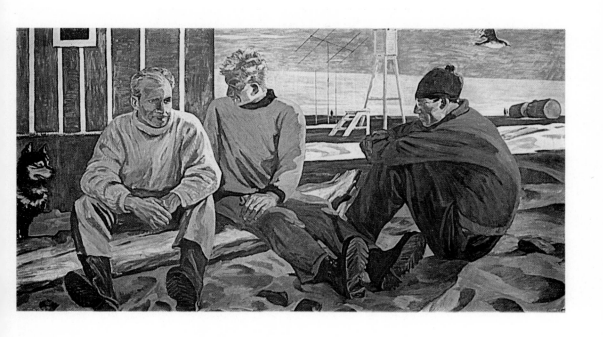

157. ALEXANDER SMOLIN, PIOTR SMOLIN
Polar Explorers. 1961

158. VIACHESLAV ZAGONEK
After the Rainstorm. 1961

159. VALENTIN SIDOROV
Children Playing Football by the Old Barns. 1975

160. VICTOR IVANOV
A Family. The Year 1945. 1964

161. ANDREI MYLNIKOV
Sisters. 1967

1 Archangel Gabriel (Angel with
Golden Hair). 12th century
Egg tempera on panel. 48 × 39*

2 The Miracle of St George. Novgorod
school. Last quarter of the 15th century
Egg tempera on panel. 58 × 41.5

3 The Presentation in the Temple.
Novgorod school. First half of the
14th century
Egg tempera on panel. 91 × 66

4 The Descent into Limbo. 1502—3
Dionysius' workshop
Egg tempera on panel. 148.9 × 113.5

5 The Old Testament Trinity. Novgorod
school. Mid-16th century
Egg tempera on panel. 148.9 × 113.5

6 Portrait of Prince Ivan Repnin. Second
half of the 17th century
Oil on canvas. 181 × 128

7 UNKNOWN ARTIST.
Active first quarter of the 18th century
Portrait of Andrei Apraxin, Peter the
Great's Jester
Oil on canvas. 93 × 88

8 IVAN NIKITIN. C. 1680—not before 1742
Portrait of Sergei Stroganov. 1726
Oil on canvas. 87 × 65

* *All measurements are given in centimetres.*

9 ROMAN NIKITIN. 1608—1753
Portrait of Maria Stroganova. Between
1721 and 1724
Oil on canvas. 111 × 90

10 ANDREI MATVEYEV. 1701—1739
Self-Portrait of the Artist with His
Wife. 1729 (?)
Oil on canvas. 75.5 × 90.5

11 IVAN NIKITIN. C. 1680—not before 1742
Portrait of Peter I. First half of the
1720s
Oil on canvas. 55 × 55 (tondo)

12 IVAN ARGUNOV. 1727—1802
Portrait of Ekaterina Lobanova-
Rostovskaya. 1754
Oil on canvas. 81.5 × 62.5

13 ALEXEI ANTROPOV. 1716—1795
Portrait of Fiodor Krasnoshchokov.
1761
Oil on canvas. 61 × 48.5

14 IVAN ARGUNOV. 1727—1802
Portrait of an Unknown Sculptor
(Architect?). 1760s
Oil on canvas. 83.5 × 64 (oval)

15 IVAN VISHNIAKOV. 1699—1761
Portrait of Sarah-Eleanor Fermore.
1750s
Oil on canvas. 138 × 114.5

16 FIODOR ROKOTOV. 1730s—1808
Portrait of Ivan Orlov. Between
1762 and 1765
Oil on canvas. 58.5 × 46.5

33 KARL BRIULLOV. 1799—1852
Portrait of Countess Julia Samoilova
Leaving the Ball. Not later than 1842
Oil on canvas. 249 × 176

34 FIODOR BRUNI. 1799—1875
Death of Camilla, Sister of Horatius.
1824
Oil on canvas. 350 × 526.5

35 KARL BRIULLOV. 1799—1852
The Last Day of Pompeii. 1833
Oil on canvas. 456.5 × 651

36 VASILY TROPININ. 1776—1857
The Solitary Guitar Player (Portrait
of Pavel Vasilyev). 1830s
Oil on canvas. 95 × 75

37 OREST KIPRENSKY. 1782—1836
Portrait of Karl Albrecht. 1827
Oil on canvas. 196.5 × 138.5

38 ALEXEI VENETSIANOV. 1780—1847
Girl with a Birch-bark Jar. C. 1824
Oil on panel. 29.5 × 23.5

39 ALEXEI VENETSIANOV. 1780—1847
Sleeping Shepherd-boy. Between
1823 and 1826
Oil on panel. 27.5 × 36.5

40 GRIGORY SOROKA. 1823—1864
The Study in a Country House at
Ostrovki. 1844
Oil on canvas. 54 × 65

41 NIKIFOR KRYLOV. 1802—1831
Winter Landscape (Russian Winter).
1827
Oil on canvas. 54 × 63.5

42 PAVEL FEDOTOV. 1815—1852
Portrait of Nadezhda Zhdanovich at
the Piano. 1849
Oil on canvas. 24.5 × 19.2

43 PAVEL FEDOTOV. 1815—1852
The Major's Marriage Proposal. 1851
Oil on canvas. 56 × 76

44 IVAN AIVAZOVSKY. 1817—1900
View of Odessa on a Moonlit Night.
1846
Oil on canvas. 122 × 190

45 IVAN AIVAZOVSKY. 1817—1900
The Brig *Mercury*. 1848
Oil on canvas. 123.5 × 190

46 ALEXANDER IVANOV. 1806—1858
Tree in the Shadow above the Water
in the Vicinity of Castel Gandolfo.
Not earlier than 1846
Oil on paper mounted on canvas. 45 × 58.2

47 ALEXANDER IVANOV. 1806—1858
Three Naked Boys. 1840—50s
Study for the painting *Christ Appearing
before the People*. 1833—57
Oil on canvas. 47.7 × 64.5 cm

48 ALEXANDER IVANOV. 1806—1558
Head of John the Baptist. Study for the
painting *Christ Appearing before the
People*. 1833—57
Oil on paper mounted on canvas. 64.2 × 58

49 NIKOLAI GAY. 1831—1894
The Last Supper. 1863
Oil on canvas. 283 × 382

50 IVAN KRAMSKOI. 1837—1887
Portrait of the Sculptor Mark
Antokolsky. 1876
Oil on canvas. 75 × 63.5

51 NIKOLAI GAY. 1831—1894
Peter the Great Interrogating
Tsarevich Alexei in Peterhof. 1872
Replica of the 1871 painting of the
same name
Oil on canvas. 134.5 × 173

52 IVAN KRAMSKOI. 1837—1887
Mina Moiseyev. 1882. Study for the
painting of 1883, *Peasant with a Bridle*
Oil on canvas. 57 × 45

53 IVAN KRAMSKOI. 1837—1887
Portrait of the Painter Ivan Shishkin.
1880
Oil on canvas. 115.5 × 83.5

54 ALEXEI SAVRASOV. 1830—1897
View of the Moscow Kremlin. Spring.
1873
Oil on canvas. 46 × 36.8

55 FIODOR VASILYEV. 1850—1873
The Thaw. 1871
Replica of the 1871 painting of the
same name
Oil on canvas. 55.5 × 108.5

56 FIODOR VASILYEV. 1850—1873
Scene on the Volga. Barques. 1870
Oil on canvas. 67 × 105

57 GRIGORY MIASOYEDOV. 1834—1911
The Mowers. 1887
Oil on canvas. 179 × 275

58 VASILY PEROV. 1834—1882
A Meal in the Monastery. 1865—76
Oil on canvas. 84 × 126

59 LEONID SOLOMATKIN. 1837—1883
Petrouchka. 1878
Oil on canvas. 29 × 22

60 ARKHIP KUINJI. 1842 (?)—1910
Evening in the Ukraine. 1878. Partially
repainted in 1901
Oil on canvas. 81 × 163

61 IVAN SHISHKIN. 1832—1898
Mast-tree Grove. 1898
Oil on canvas. 165 × 252

62 ISAAC LEVITAN. 1860—1900
Golden Autumn. Village. 1889.
Partially repainted in 1898
Oil on canvas. 43 × 67.2

63 ISAAC LEVITAN. 1860—1900
The Lake. Russia. 1899—1900
Oil on canvas. 149 × 208

64 ISAAC LEVITAN. 1860—1900
Meadow on the Edge of a Forest. 1898
Pastel on paper. 63.5 × 49

65 VASILY POLENOV. 1844—1927
In the Park. The Village of Veules
in Normandy. 1874
Oil on canvas. 61 × 46

66 VASILY POLENOV. 1844—1927
Christ and the Woman Sinner. 1888
Oil on canvas. 325 × 611

67 VASILY VERESHCHAGIN. 1842—1904
The Shinto Temple in Nikko. 1903
Oil on canvas. 45 × 61

68 VASILY SURIKOV. 1848—1916
The Taking of a Snow Fortress. 1891
Oil on canvas. 156 × 282

69 VASILY SURIKOV. 1848—1916
Suvorov's Army Crossing the Alps
in 1799. 1899
Oil on canvas. 459 × 373

70 ILYA REPIN. 1844—1930
Portrait of Vladimir Stasov, Music
and Art Critic. 1883
Oil on canvas. 74 × 60

71 ILYA REPIN. 1844—1930
Portrait of the Cellist Alexander
Verzhbilovich. 1895
Oil on canvas. 87 × 58

72 ILYA REPIN. 1844—1930
The Volga Barge Haulers. 1870—73
Oil on canvas. 131.5 × 281

73 ILYA REPIN. 1844—1930
The Zaporozhye Cossacks Writing
a Mocking Letter to the Turkish
Sultan. 1880—91
Oil on canvas. 203 × 358

74 ILYA REPIN. 1844—1930
Portrait of Konstantin Pobedonostsev.
Study for the painting
The State Council in Formal Session.
1903
Oil on canvas. 68.5 × 53

75 VALENTIN SEROV. 1865—1911
Children. 1899
Oil on canvas. 71 × 54

76 VALENTIN SEROV. 1865—1911
Portrait of Felix Yusupov. 1903
Oil on canvas. 89 × 71.5

77 VALENTIN SEROV. 1865—1911
Portrait of Sophia Botkina. 1899
Oil on canvas. 189 × 139.5

78 KONSTANTIN SOMOV. 1869—1939
Portrait of Anna Ostroumova. 1901
Oil on canvas. 87 × 63

79 MIKHAIL NESTEROV. 1862—1942
Portrait of Olga Nesterova, the Artist's
Daughter. 1906
Oil on canvas. 175 × 86.5

80 MIKHAIL VRUBEL. 1856—1910
The Bogatyr. Decorative panel. 1898
Oil on canvas. 321.5 × 222

81 MIKHAIL VRUBEL. 1856—1910
Six-winged Seraph. 1904
Oil on canvas. 131 × 155

82 LEON BAKST. 1866—1924
Portrait of Sergei Diaghilev with His
Nurse. 1906
Oil on canvas. 161 × 116

83 MIKHAIL NESTEROV. 1862—1942
The Taking of the Veil. 1898
Oil on canvas. 178 × 195

84 KONSTANTIN KOROVIN. 1861—1939
The Harbour in Gurzuf. 1914
Oil on canvas. 89 × 121

85 KONSTANTIN KOROVIN. 1861—1939
Portrait of the Actress Tatyana
Liubatovich
Oil on canvas. 160 × 84

86 VICTOR BORISOV-MUSATOV. 1870—1905
Self-Portrait of the Artist with His
Sister. 1898
Oil on canvas. 143 × 177

87 VICTOR BORISOV-MUSATOV. 1870—1905
Spring. 1901
Oil on canvas. 71 × 98

88 EVGENY LANCERAY. 1875—1946
St Petersburg in the Early Eighteenth
Century. 1906
Tempera on paper. 58.5 × 111.5

89 KONSTANTIN SOMOV. 1869—1939
Winter. Skating-rink. 1915
Oil on canvas. 49 × 58

90 KONSTANTIN YUON. 1875—1958
The St Trinity Lavra in Winter. 1910
Oil on canvas. 125 × 198

91 PHILIP MALIAVIN. 1869—1940
Two Peasant Women. 1905
Oil on canvas. 205 × 159

92 ANDREI RIABUSHKIN. 1861—1904
A Seventeenth-century Moscow Street
on a Holiday. 1895
Oil on canvas. 204 × 390

93 ABRAM ARKHIPOV. 1862—1930
A Festive Day in Spring (On a Visit).
1915. A version of the 1914 picture
of the same name
Oil on canvas. 105 × 154

94 APOLLINARY VASNETSOV. 1856—1933
Seventeenth-century Moscow. Street
in Kitai-gorod. 1900
Oil on canvas. 125 × 178

95 VICTOR VASNETSOV. 1848—1926
Vitiaz (Knight) at the Crossroads. 1882
Oil on canvas. 167 × 299

96 NIKOLAI ROERICH. 1874—1947
Slavs on the Dnieper. 1905
Tempera on cardboard. 67 × 89

97 NIKOLAI ROERICH. 1874—1947
St Prokopius. 1914
Tempera on cardboard. 70 × 105

98 ALEXANDER GOLOVIN. 1863—1930
A Street in Seville. Sketch of the stage
set for Bizet's opera *Carmen*. 1906
Tempera on paper mounted on cardboard.
69 × 101

99   ALEXANDER GOLOVIN. 1863—1930
Portrait of **Fiodor Shaliapin** as Boris
Godunov in **Mussorgsky**'s opera of the
same name. 1912
Tempera and foil on canvas. 211.5 × 139.5

100   IGOR GRABAR. 1871—1960
Still Life with **Pears.** 1915
Oil on canvas. 73.5 × 60.5

101   IGOR GRABAR. 1871—1960
Flowers and **Fruit.** 1904
Oil on canvas. 79 × 101

102   ZINAIDA SEREBRIAKOVA. 1884—1967
A House of Cards. 1919
Oil on canvas. 65 × 75.5

103   ZINAIDA SEREBRIAKOVA. 1884—1967
Study of a **Girl** (Self-Portrait). 1911
Oil on canvas. 72 × 58

104   ZINAIDA SEREBRIAKOVA. 1884—1967
Peasants. 1914
Oil on canvas. 123.5 × 98

105   KUZMA PETROV-VODKIN. 1878—1939
A Mother. 1915
Oil on canvas. 107 × 98.5

106   BORIS KUSTODIEV. 1878—1927
A Merchant's Wife **Drinking** Tea. 1918
Oil on canvas. 120 × 120

107   BORIS KUSTODIEV. 1878—1927
Portrait of **Fiodor** Shaliapin. 1922
Oil on canvas. 99 × 80

108   ILYA MASHKOV. 1881—1944
Still Life with Loaves of Bread
Oil on canvas. 105 × 133

109   PIOTR KONCHALOVSKY. 1876—1956
Family Portrait. 1911
Oil on canvas. 177 × 238

110   ALEXANDER KUPRIN. 1880—1960
Still Life with Blue Fan. 1919
Oil on canvas. 115 × 120

111   NATHAN ALTMAN. 1889—1970
Portrait of Anna Akhmatova. 1914
Oil on canvas. 123.5 × 103.2

112   ROBERT FALK. 1886—1958
The Crimea. Lombardy Poplar. 1915
Oil on canvas. 108 × 88

113   MARK CHAGALL. 1887—1985
The Promenade. 1917
Oil on canvas. 170 × 163.5

114   KASIMIR MALEVICH. 1878—1935
Marpha and Van'ka. 1909—10
Oil on canvas. 82 × 61

115   DAVID STERENBERG. 1881—1948
Still Life with Oil Lamp. About 1922
Oil on cardboard. 50 × 36

116   VASILY ROZHDESTVENSKY. 1884—1963
Still Life with Red Jug. 1918
Oil on canvas. 89 × 84

117   KUZMA PETROV-VODKIN. 1878—1939
Violin. 1918
Oil on canvas. 65 × 80

118   KONSTANTIN YUON. 1875—1958
Young People of the Moscow Suburbs.
1926
Oil on canvas. 59 × 67

119 BORIS KUSTODIEV. 1878—1927
Festivities Marking the Opening of the
Second Congress of the Comintern and
Demonstration on Uritsky
(Palace) Square in Petrograd on
July 19, 1920. 1921
Oil on canvas. 133 × 268

120 FIODOR BOGORODSKY. 1895—1959
At the Photographer's. 1932
Oil on canvas. 148 × 111

121 KUZMA PETROV-VODKIN. 1878—1939
Death of a Commissar. 1928
Oil on canvas. 196 × 248

122 ARKADY RYLOV. 1870—1939
Wind in the Trees. 1904
Oil on canvas. 107 × 146

123 ARKADY RYLOV. 1870—1939
Autumn on the Tosna River. 1920
Oil on canvas. 78 × 101

124 MARTIROS SARYAN. 1880—1972
Yerevan. 1924
Oil on canvas. 68 × 68

125 MARTIROS SARYAN. 1880—1972
Hyenas. 1909
Tempera on cardboard. 67.5 × 99

126 ALEXANDER SHEVCHENKO. 1883—1948
Kurd Women. 1932—33
Oil on canvas. 121 × 98.5

127 ALEXANDER SHEVCHENKO. 1883—1948
Girl with Pears. 1933
Oil on canvas. 109 × 89

128 NIKOLAI CHERNYSHOV. 1885—1973
Young Collective Farmer (Girl with
a Kid). 1929
Oil on canvas. 96 × 60

129 PAVEL KUZNETSOV. 1878—1968
Tobacco-workers. 1925—26
Tempera and oil on canvas. 97 × 107

130 ALEXANDER SAMOKHVALOV. 1894—1971
Young Woman Worker. 1928
Oil on canvas. 65 × 50.5

131 ALEXANDER SAMOKHVALOV. 1894—1971
Weavers. 1929
Tempera and oil on canvas. 67 × 97.5

132 SERGEI GERASIMOV. 1885—1964
Autumntide. 1953
Oil on cardboard. 49.5 × 68

133 ALEXANDER GERASIMOV. 1881—1963
Midday. Warm Rain. 1939
Oil on canvas. 127 × 99

134 YURI PIMENOV. 1903—1977
Portrait of Varia Shitakova. 1935
Oil on canvas. 90.5 × 70.5

135 MIKHAIL NESTEROV. 1862—1942
Portrait of the Surgeon Sergei Yudin.
1933
Oil on canvas. 99 × 80

136 PIOTR KONCHALOVSKY. 1876—1956
The Novgorodians. 1925
Oil on canvas. 138 × 181

137 GEORGY RIAZHSKY. 1895—1952
Self-Portrait. 1928
Oil on canvas. 53 × 44 cm

138 ALEXANDER DEINEKA. 1899—1969
La Parisienne. 1935
Oil on canvas. 64 × 54

139 ALEXANDER DEINEKA. 1899—1969
Mont Vernon. The Highway. 1935
Oil on canvas. 60 × 80

140 ALEXANDER OSMIORKIN. 1892—1953
The "New Holland" Arch. 1945
Oil on canvas. 100 × 75

141 ALEXEI KAREV. 1879—1942
The Neva. 1934
Oil on canvas. 116 × 173

142 THE KUKRYNIKSY
(MIKHAIL KUPRIYANOV,
PORPHIRY KRYLOV,
NIKOLAI SOKOLOV)
MIKHAIL KUPRIYANOV. Born 1903
PORPHIRY KRYLOV. Born 1902
NIKOLAI SOKOLOV. Born 1903
The Nazis Being Routed from
Novgorod. 1944—46
Oil on canvas. 199 × 229

143 ALEXANDER DEINEKA. 1899—1969
The Defence of Sevastopol. 1942
Oil on canvas. 200 × 400

144 ARKADY PLASTOV. 1893—1972
Youth. 1954
Oil on canvas. 170 × 204

145 ARKADY PLASTOV. 1893—1972
Vitia the Shepherd-boy. 1951
Oil on canvas. 121 × 186

146 YURI PIMENOV. 1903—1977
Venice. A Lonely Flower Girl. 1958
Oil on canvas mounted on cardboard.
48 × 40

147 YURI PIMENOV. 1903—1977
Trend-setters of a New District. From
the *New District* series. 1961
Oil on canvas. 71 × 80

148 SEMION CHUIKOV. 1902—1980
The Song of a Coolie. Central panel
of the triptych *Simple People of India*.
1959
Oil on canvas. 137 × 170

149 SEMION CHUIKOV. 1902—1980
Morning in a Mountain Village. 1967
Oil on canvas. 118 × 179

150 GEORGY NISSKY. 1903—1987
Above the Snows. 1960
Oil on canvas. 100 × 186

151 PAVEL KORIN. 1892—1967
Portrait of Renato Guttuso. 1961
Oil on canvas. 115 × 112

152 EVSEI MOISEYENKO. Born 1916
Cherries. 1969
Oil on canvas. 187 × 275

153 EVSEI MOISEYENKO. Born 1916
Victory. 1970—72
Oil on canvas. 200 × 150

ГОСУДАРСТВЕННЫЙ РУССКИЙ МУЗЕЙ, ЛЕНИНГРАД
ЖИВОПИСЬ

Альбом (на английском языке)

Автор-составитель Николай Николаевич Новоуспенский
Художник Б. Осенчаков
Редакторы Е. Яковишина, О. Пирумова
Редактор английского текста Ю. Памфилов
Художественный редактор Т. Иванова-Бойцова
Технические редакторы Н. Голубева, В. Кленова
Корректор Е. Харькова

ИБ № 2925. Сдано в набор 06.03.87. Подписано в печать 25.07.88. Формат $70 \times 75^1/_{16}$
Бумага мелованная. Гарнитура обыкновенная. Высокая печать
Усл. печ. л. 11,64. Усл. кр.-отт. 58,81. Уч.-изд. л. 9,68
Тираж 50 000. Заказ Т3108. Изд. № 1633. Цена 4 р. 30 к.
Издательство „Аврора". 191065, Ленинград, Невский пр., 7/9
Ленинградская типография № 3 Головное предприятие
дважды ордена Трудового Красного Знамени Ленинградского производственного
объединения «Типография имени Ивана Федорова» Союзполиграфпрома
при Государственном комитете СССР по делам издательств, полиграфии
и книжной торговли. 191126, Ленинград, Звенигородская ул., 11

ГОСУДАРСТВЕННЫЙ РУССКИЙ МУЗЕЙ, ЛЕНИНГРАД

ЖИВОПИСЬ

Альбом (на английском языке)

Автор-составитель Николай Николаевич Новоуспенский
Художник Б. Осенчаков
Редакторы Е. Яковишина, О. Пирумова
Редактор английского текста Ю. Памфилов
Художественный редактор Т. Иванова-Бойцова
Технические редакторы Н. Голубева, В. Кленова
Корректор Е. Харькова

ИБ № 2925. Сдано в набор 06.03.87. Подписано в печать 25.07.88. Формат $70 \times 75^1/_{16}$
Бумага мелованная. Гарнитура обыкновенная. Высокая печать
Усл. печ. л. 11,64. Усл. кр.-отт. 58,81. Уч.-изд. л. 9,68
Тираж 50 000. Заказ Т3108. Изд. № 1633. Цена 4 р. 30 к.
Издательство „Аврора". 191065, Ленинград, Невский пр., 7/9
Ленинградская типография № 3 Головное предприятие
дважды ордена Трудового Красного Знамени Ленинградского производственного
объединения «Типография имени Ивана Федорова» Союзполиграфпрома
при Государственном комитете СССР по делам издательств, полиграфии
и книжной торговли. 191126, Ленинград, Звенигородская ул., 11